Where Is Sanitiy?

Marguerite Danby

Presentation by *BookLeaf Publishing*

Web: www.bookleafpub.com

E-mail: info@bookleafpub.com

ISBN: 9789357441117

First edition 2023

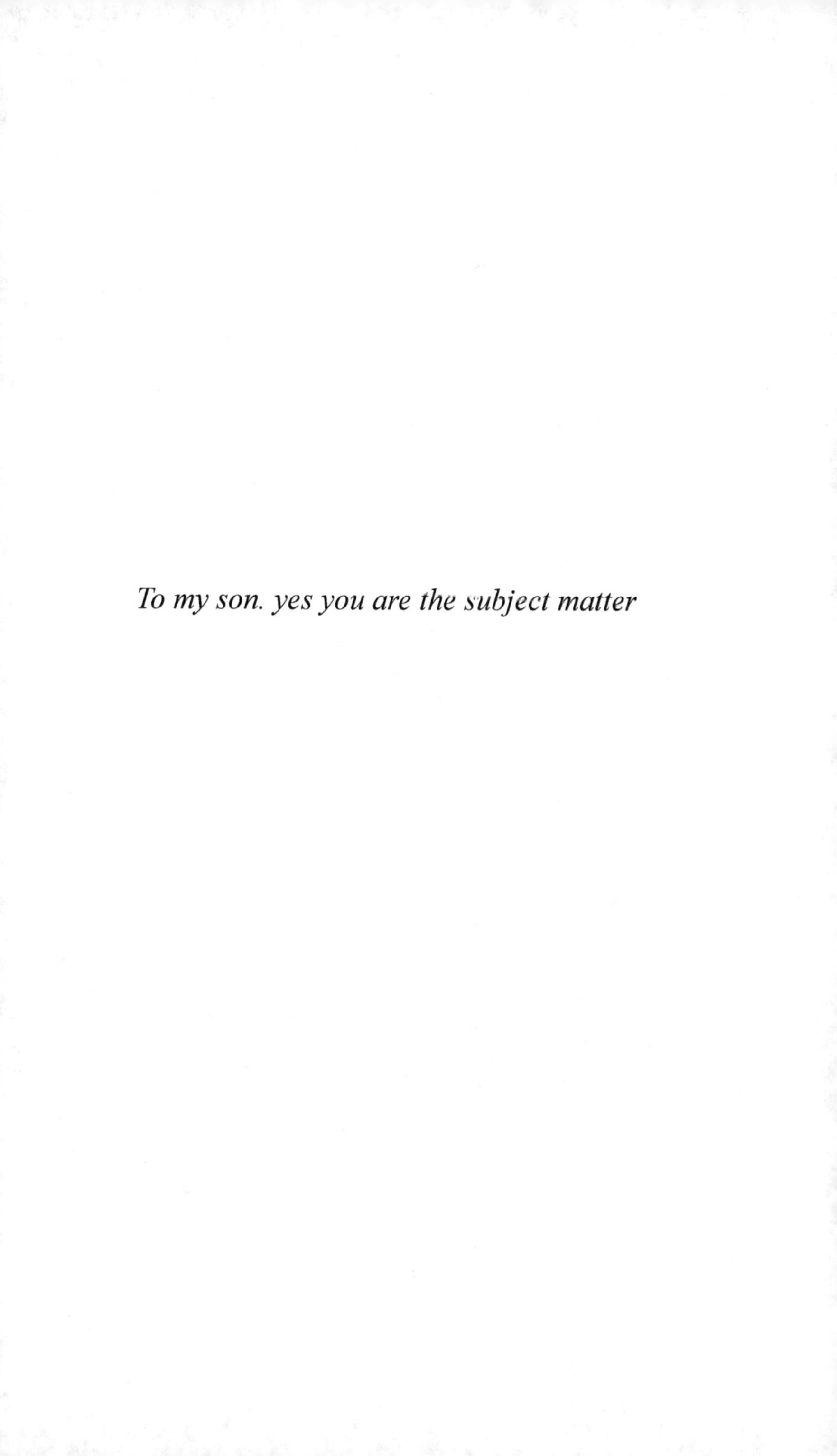

To my son. yes you are the subject matter

ACKNOWLEDGEMENT

I would like to thank my mother for inspiring me, my husband for supporting me, and bookleaf for this opportunity as well as all the ladies I work with for giving me so much material

Where is Sanity

Very hairy hair
It stares creepily
where is sanity

My Day

Quiet calm
Quiet happy
Quiet where
Quiet Scared
Quiet worried
Quiet what's going on
Quest mess
Quiet clean
Quiet Sleep
Quiet Happy
Quiet Calm

looking back

3

Sweet sanity you due elude me
for where else will I get my poetry
and let us have this thought
that you and I are not
as much much different as i would like
for you are just a little tyke
with hope and dreams and memories
that will set the world at ease

games

creepers creep down low
towers touch the sky up high
in the middle fly

songs

5

songs dance, prance, and, sing
let them take wing
so that they can bring
happiness and job while they sing

Imagination

May the mermaid shine and glow
bringing the sparkle back to the eyes dulled by
the burden of expectation

May the Ocean call
bringing back the wonder stolen by the eternal
slog

May childhood never look forward
and say no that's not ok with the idea of
responsibility

May magic happen

just out of step

just out of step
a little out of sink
just out of step
not quite on the same page
just out of step
what does it even mean why can't we seem to
agree
Are you spinning out of focus
why can't we aline
I feel like all my time
is used on trying to see inside your mind
just out of step
a little out of sink
just out of step
not quite on the same page
just out of step
what does it even mean why can't we seem to
agree
Maybe we need
to try and understand
just because we're similar
sosnt mean we're the same
why much we be the same to agree
dont you know how hard that is to be
just out of step

a little out of sink
just out of step
not quite on the same page
just out of step
what does it even mean why can't we seem to
agree
i just want there to be you and me

why

9

songs in my crazed mind
they dance round and round in my
Dreams in my crazed head

birth

In and out Deeply
A sign of change new as spring
Welcome on and all

simple

Simple wishes
simple dreams
simple hopes
simple fears
simple smiles
simple tears
simple songs
simple dance
simple stories
simple chance
but what is not simple at all
is when life takes you very far

Life

why must everything
go in
a
cycle of
everything and nothing

childhood

13

their eyes full of hope
reaching out to hold tight to
the changing springtime

oops

My body came up with the idea
My heart set itself without delay
But my logical head always loses
cause I don't know when I should listen

Tea

Oh Cherry blossoms
Beneath the azure sky Why
do you lie about sweetness

color

The window to the
soal where seen is emotion
brilliant color

see

These tired Feet see
they've gone up and down see
just to see the sea

art

what is a true piece
of art from an artist's hand
go stroke after stroke

change

19

bleeding heart in time
to the music of all life
listen listen now?

adventure

In the Jungle light
swinging on a beam of light
so very far to go

clean

Clean but never clean
deeply pungent
the eyes sting
let me bring
healthy bring
how much we sing
now keep it clean
slumber sleepy head
then do it al over again

bedtime

This song on my lips
It winds its way round and round
around the world hush